A New True Book

OIL SPILLS

By Darlene R. Stille

CHILDRENS PRESS ®
CHICAGO

An oil spill off the coast of France

PHOTO CREDITS

AP/Wide World Photos—13, 17, 19, 27 (2 photos), 28, 30, 31, 44 (bottom)

© Camerique—45

H. Armstrong Roberts—43

Journalism Services—© Dirk Gallian, 26

Photri—4 (2 bottom photos), 15 (top), 25, 32, 34, 40, (2 photos), 44 (top); © B. Kulik, 42

Tom Stack & Associates—© Ken W. Davis, 22, 36 (left); © David M. Dennis, 36 (right)

SuperStock International, Inc.—8; © Ernest Manewal, 4 (top left); © George Glod, 9, 11; © D.C. Lowe, 10; © Audrey Ross, 14; © Dwayne Harlan, 15 (bottom); © Jack Novak, 39

Third Coast Stock Source—© Jeff Lowe, 24

TSW/CLICK-Chicago—© Martin Rogers, Cover, 2, 18, 38; © Peter Menzel, 21

Valan—© Stephen J. Krasemann, 4 (top right), 20 (right); © Jean Bruneau, 6 (right); © Kennon Cooke, 6 (left); © K Ghani, 20 (left)

COVER: Oil spill in Brittany, France

Library of Congress Cataloging-in-Publication Data

Stille, Darlene R.
    Oil spills / by Darlene R. Stille.
        p.   cm. — (A New true book)
    Includes index.
    Summary: Describes how oil spills occur, the damage they cause to the environment, cleanup operations, and ways to prevent oil spills.
    ISBN 0-516-01116-2
    1. Oil spills—Environmental aspects—Juvenile literature. 2. Oil pollution of water—Juvenile literature. [1. Oil spills. 2. Water—Pollution. 3. Pollution.] I. Title.
TD427.P4S69   1991   90-21455
363.73'82—dc20   CIP
                                         AC

TABLE OF CONTENTS

Oil runs through pipes to heat houses in Alaska (above).
Oil is made into fuel for boats, automobiles, and jet planes.

OIL IS IMPORTANT

Oil, or petroleum, is an important source of energy in the modern world. Many types of fuel are made from oil.

Heating oil keeps houses warm. Gasoline makes autos run. Ships, trains, trucks, and jet planes all use fuel made from oil.

The process of making fuels and other chemicals from oil is called refining.

The paint, the synthetic clothing, and the plastic hard hat that these men are using all come from oil products.

Many products we use in our homes are made from refined oil. Paints, plastics, synthetic clothing, even some medicines are made of chemicals refined from oil.

Oil is very useful and important. But if oil spills into the environment, it can cause great harm.

WHAT CAUSES OIL SPILLS?

Oil spills may happen when oil is moved from one place to another.

Oil is found underground in Alaska, California, Texas, Oklahoma, and other states. There is also oil in Russia, the North Sea, and South America. But most of the world's oil comes from the Middle East.

Oil drilled from wells is called crude oil. It must be

An oil refinery in Edmonton, Canada

sent to refineries, where it
can be made into fuels and
chemicals. From the

refineries, it is sent to places
that need the refined oil.
Sometimes the oil is sent
through pipelines. Often it is

An oil pipeline may run for hundreds
of miles, passing over hills and rivers.

A giant supertanker is serviced in Portland, Oregon.
These ships are the largest ever built.

A tanker takes on oil from a pipe that runs out from the shore.

carried in huge ships called oil tankers. Some oil tankers are as long as three football fields.

While crude or refined oil is being shipped, it can be spilled. A leak in a pipeline can cause an oil spill. But the most common cause is an accident to an oil tanker.

HOW AN OIL SPILL LOOKS

Most oil spills happen when tankers are damaged at sea. A tanker could be damaged by an explosion or fire. A tanker could run aground in shallow water. It could strike a rock.

These accidents rip open the side or bottom of the ship, called the hull. The oil pours out of the ship's hull into the sea.

This tanker was wrecked off the coast of France in 1978.
The brown stain in the water is a spreading oil slick.

Oil is lighter than water.
So oil floats on the surface
of the sea.

Sticky black oil must be scraped from the rocks on the seashore.

The oil spreads across the water. This is called an oil slick. It can wash up on beaches, coating the sand and rocks with sticky black goo. Wherever the oil spreads, it kills plants and animals.

A sinking ship (above) spills oil into the sea. When the oil slick reaches shore, workers (below) gather to clean the mess from the beach.

OIL IS A POISON

Oil is poisonous to all kinds of plants and animals. But some kinds of oil are more poisonous than others.

This is because oil contains many different chemicals. The chemical mix determines how poisonous a type of oil is.

Crude oil is usually the least poisonous type of oil. Refined oil is much more poisonous. Even a small amount of highly poisonous

OTHER WAYS OIL CAUSES HARM

Oil can kill in other ways. It can coat birds and sea mammals.

When a bird's feathers are coated with oil, the bird cannot fly. Also, a bird's

A Saudi Arabian official examines a bird killed by the massive oil spill in the Persian Gulf that came from oil deliberately leaked into the gulf by Iraq during its illegal occupation of Kuwait in 1991.

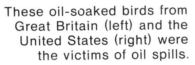
These oil-soaked birds from Great Britain (left) and the United States (right) were the victims of oil spills.

feathers keep it warm. But when the feathers are coated with oil, the bird can freeze to death.

Seals, sea otters, and other sea mammals have fur that keeps them warm in cold water. When they are coated with oil, they can freeze to death.

Oil in the water can also kill seaweed, which many animals use as food.

This oil-coated seaweed will die, and many animals will lose a source of food.

Oil-cleanup workers remove a snare used to catch oil on a beach.

CLEANING UP SPILLED OIL

There is no easy way to clean up an oil spill. Some of the oil can be cleaned up by workers. But the rest of the oil must be cleaned up by nature.

Nature cleans up oil by evaporation. Some of the oil in a slick turns to vapor and mixes with the air.

There are also natural bacteria in sea water that eat oil.

Workers can use a kind of floating "fence" to keep the oil slick from spreading. These fences are called booms. They look like giant links of sausages.

A cleanup crew at work in Prince William Sound, Alaska

Workers vacuum oil from a boom.

Cleanup crews also use
special boats called skimmers.
Skimmers vacuum the oil
off the surface.

But it is impossible to
scoop up all the oil. Nature
must finish the cleanup.

A cleanup crew places oil-contaminated material in plastic bags on a California beach.

CLEANING UP BEACHES

Cleanup is harder if the oil washes up on a beach or into a marsh. The oil coats everything it touches.

The birds and mammals covered with oil must be

An oil-soaked bird gets a bath with a toothbrush (left). Only a small number of affected birds can be saved in this way. Oil is scrubbed from seashore rocks (right) by hand.

cleaned. Workers gather up the animals that are still alive and give them a bath.

To clean beaches, workers often use rags to wipe each rock. They also shovel up sand that is soaked in oil and carry it away.

27

High-pressure hoses remove surface oil, but they
may wash the oil deep into the sand on the shore.

But cleanup efforts sometimes make the oil damage worse. The high-pressure hoses sometimes used to wash beaches can drive the oil deeper down into the sand. Then it might slowly leak into the water for years.

Finally, all the oil-soaked rags and the clothes of the cleanup crew create a garbage problem. They must be either burned or buried.

A Saudi Arabian official checks a pool of oil on the shore of the Persian Gulf.
The 1991 gulf oil spill threatened the machinery that turns salt water
into fresh water for the people of the area.

Thousands of cormorants and other birds were killed by the Persian Gulf oil spill.

THE WORST OIL SPILLS

Some oil spills are worse than others. The longer an oil spill lasts, the more damage it is likely to do.

How long the oil stays in the water depends on several things. One is the type of oil.

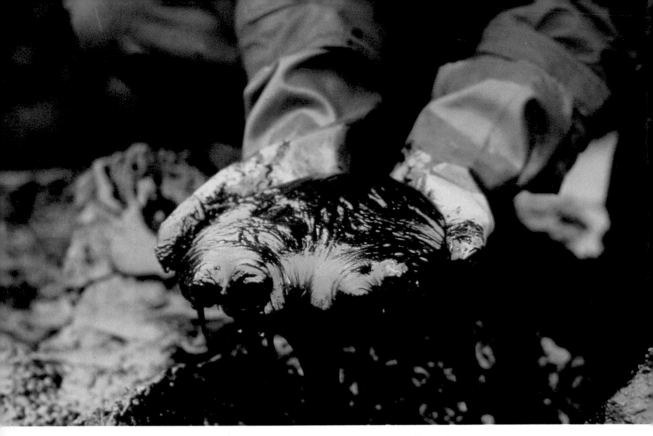

Thick crude oil from the Prince William Sound, Alaska, oil spill.

Crude oil is heavy and thick. It does not evaporate easily. Refined oil is thinner and evaporates faster. But refined oil is usually more poisonous than crude oil.

The longer oil stays in the water, the more oil will sink to the bottom. Oil that sinks to the sea bottom can stay there and cause harm for many years.

Weather is also important. Cold weather can make an oil spill worse. In cold water,

Oil pours into the sea from the damaged hull of a huge tanker.

oil evaporates more slowly.
Also, bacteria eat oil more
slowly in cold water than in
warm water.

Strong winds can spread
an oil slick for miles. High

waves will mix the oil with water. This creates something called mousse. It looks like the dessert, chocolate mousse. Mousse is very hard to clean up.

Even the time of year is important. At times when there are many young plants and animals, an oil spill has worse effects. Oil is more poisonous to young things.

Long booms (left) and absorbent pads (right)
are used on beaches to soak up the oil.

SCIENCE AND OIL SPILLS

Scientists are trying to learn more about oil spills. They want to know how much damage an oil spill can do and how long it takes the environment to recover.

But oil spills are very difficult to study. This is because each oil spill is so different.

Scientists use this test tank to study oil spills.

Also, the ocean is vast. Scientists are just beginning to learn about many parts of the ocean and its life.

Oil spills often happen in places that scientists have

not yet studied very well. So they cannot tell exactly how much damage the spill has caused.

Scientists are looking for better ways to clean up oil spills. They are experimenting with chemicals that break up oil. They are looking for better oil-eating bacteria.

A tugboat sprays detergent into an oil spill. Detergent can break up oil just as it breaks up grease in dishwater.

Pollution investigators examine oil that has washed ashore
(left) and take samples from a floating oil boom.

But scientists who study
oil spills do not believe that
any spill can be cleaned up
completely. All oil spills will
do some damage to the
environment.

PREVENTING OIL SPILLS

Scientists believe that the best way to deal with oil spills is to keep them from happening.

Safer ships could be built. These ships would have two hulls, one inside the other. If the outer hull was damaged, the inner hull would still hold the oil.

There could be better ways to guide ships through narrow, shallow, or rocky

Tugboats guide huge ships through narrow or dangerous ocean passages.

passages. Tugboats could pull the giant tankers. Radar on the ship and on the shore could help the captains steer the ships.

Governments could make it illegal to build pipelines or to ship oil in places that could suffer serious environmental damage. These easily damaged environments are usually in cold climates. Alaska and Antarctica are places that could be badly damaged by oil spills.

Tankers take on crude oil at the end of the Alaska pipeline in Valdez.

An oil spill
begins (above). An
oil-damaged heron
(left) perches near
a pier after
diving into an
oil slick near
Galveston, Texas.

A tanker heads out to sea with its dangerous cargo.

If there were no oil shipments, there would be no oil spills. But this is not possible. The modern world runs on oil. So people must find new ways to ship oil safely.

WORDS YOU SHOULD KNOW

bacteria (back • TEER • ee • yah) — tiny living things that have only one cell and that can be seen only with a microscope

chemicals (KEM • ih • kilz) — materials that are used in many manufacturing processes and that are often harmful to living things

environment (en • VY • run • ment) — all the things that surround us on the earth; air, soil, water, etc.

evaporation (ee • vap • er • RAY • shun) — the change of a material from a solid or liquid to a gaseous state

marsh (MAHRSH) — low land that is covered with shallow water

mousse (MOOSE) — a light, spongy substance somewhat like heavy whipped cream

petroleum (peh • TROH • lee • um) — crude oil that is found in the earth; the liquid remains of plants and animals that lived long ago

pipeline (PYP • line) — a long line of connected pipes used to move liquids such as oil

poisonous (POY • zun • niss) — containing poison; causing sickness or death if eaten

radar (RAY • dahr) — a device that finds objects by bouncing radio waves off them

refinery (rih • FYN • er • ree) — a place where crude oil is made into gasoline and other fuels

seaweed (SEE • weed) — plants that live in water

synthetic (sin • THET • ick) — not natural; made by people

vapor (VAY • per) — a gas formed when a liquid or solid substance is heated

INDEX

About the Author

Darlene R. Stille is a Chicago-based science writer and editor.